W9-CSG-029

CHOICES

WHO WILL YOU SERVE?

STEVE MAYS

Copyright © 2005 by Steve Mays

Published by Word for Life, Gardena, CA

All rights reserved. No part of this publication may be reproduced, stored in a retrieval system, or transmitted in any form or by any means without the prior permission of the publisher, except as provided by USA copyright law.

All Scripture quotations, unless otherwise indicated, are taken from the *New King James Version*®. Copyright © 1982 by Thomas Nelson, Inc. Used by permission. All rights reserved.

ISBN 0-9761478-0-7

Printed in the United States of America

Dedication

I would like to dedicate this humble work to my greatest friend, constant encourager, best student, and lovely wife, Gail. She has been and continues to be "a little piece of heaven" in my life and our children's lives. Also to Pastor Chuck and Kay Smith, for without them, I would have never been taught the importance of loving God's Word and His people.

TABLE OF CONTENTS

INTRODUCTION

Choices . . . life is full of them. Not a day goes by in which we don't have to make some kind of decision. It may be as simple as when to eat or what to wear. Or it may be as difficult as choosing a job, career, or your future mate. But, whatever the case, no one is exempt from choices.

Having been a pastor for more than 30 years, I have personally witnessed the devastating effects of bad choices: A teenager racing down the streets of Los Angeles one minute, the next minute gone forever in a horrible crash, all because of a foolish choice. A marriage destroyed, ending in a bitter divorce, all because two people refuse to express to one another what they feel inside. Foolishly they choose to hide their feelings rather than save their marriage. Two business acquaintances, one a believer and the other a nonbeliever, make a decision to go into business together. Yet the new venture fails and the friendship is shattered forever, beyond repair, all because the believer made a foolish choice to be unequally yoked in business.

Similar stories can be multiplied by the thousands. It is likely that you have tried to help pick up the pieces of broken hearts and lives of family and friends, shattered due to bad choices. Yet you might also remember a time when someone else helped you rebound from the consequences of a bad choice you had made.

Many times our bad choices are a result of simply wanting things our way. We choose to keep God out of our decision-making process. We ignore all of the roadblocks and warning signs of divine intervention that God puts in our path. I have been told, "But Pastor Steve, you have no idea what I have been through!" That is absolutely right. But God does! He has been waiting a long time for each one of us to choose to surrender our will and life to Him. His way is best, and it always leads us to a more intimate relationship with Him.

Personal bad choices affect our past, present, and future. So many people today are hurting in incredible ways from past decisions that were made without ever considering the impact they would have on their life. Many people today despise their present situation because in what was perhaps a moment of weakness, they made a choice that they are now bearing the consequences of and will continue to do so well into the future.

I cannot emphasize enough the importance of making good and godly choices! Your choices must be made and understood in the light of Scripture. They have nothing to do with culture, circumstances, or even current events. They have everything to do with your relationship with and knowledge of God. When your devotional life is strong, your relationship with the Lord will be strong and you will hear His Spirit speak very clearly to you through His Word. This removes any guesswork from your choices. However, when your spiritual life is wavering, you will have a difficult time discerning what the will of God is, and in the end you will make wrong choices.

God has so much planned for you, but He will not remove your freedom to make choices. I can't emphasize enough that the choices you make today will shape your tomorrows. As you read through this booklet, I pray that the Holy Spirit will stir your heart, mind, and soul to be obedient to the will of God. May it challenge you to make choices in light of what God wants for you and not according to your flesh or your own strength.

Let's admit it, life can be a difficult thing to survive, especially being your own worst enemy. You can try to blame your issues on society, culture, the media, your education, or even your parents. But time and again, I have seen that the root problem for most people is wrong choices. God has a way for us to go. The world has a way too. Instead of making a break with the world and choosing God, many try to live somewhere in between. They choose to split their devotion and end up serving two masters: God and this world.

The Bible clearly deals with the problem of not choosing God wholeheartedly. You cannot serve God and the treasures of this world. Matthew 6:24 reads, "No one can serve two masters; for either he will hate the one and love the other, or else he will be loyal to the one and despise the other. You cannot serve God and mammon [the treasures of the world]."

Imagine a husband telling both his wife and his mistress how much he loves and needs them in his life. You may balk at this thought—and should—but there are husbands who have said (and done) this to their wives, believing that such split devotion is legitimate or at least not damaging as long as it's kept hidden. Such a man is lying to himself. He cannot be devoted to two people at the same time and love them equally. Sooner or later, his two interests will clash, and he *will* have to choose one over the other.

Many Christians, similarly, rationalize that they can have two lovers. They decide to straddle the fence, trying to live the Christian life while embracing the things of the world. And I can tell you, without a doubt, this doesn't work! It's as ridiculous as the man who thinks he can have both a wife and a mistress. If a person chooses to try to serve both God and worldly pleasure, he will end up compromising his Christian values and beliefs. Before long, he will be completely absorbed in the behaviors and attitudes of the world.

This struggle with split devotion is not a new problem. First Kings 18:21 says, "And Elijah came to all the people, and said, 'How long will you falter between two opinions? If the LORD is God, follow Him; but if Baal [the false god of pleasure], follow him.' " In other words, make your choice because you can't waver between two masters.

Take a look at your life right now. Think for a moment about your daily choices. What is it that you spend most of your time doing? Whatever gets the majority of your time and attention reveals what or whom you love the most. Are your devotions split between many things? Do you find yourself looking for happiness or security in the things of this world such as money, friends, your career, or perhaps even your appearance? Or can you honestly say that God is the source of your joy and the focus of your attention?

I wrote this booklet in an effort to help you understand how important your day-to-day choices are. You can choose the world, or you can choose God. You can choose to hate, or you can go God's way and choose to love. You can get angry and bitter for some unfair thing done to you, or you can choose God's way and forgive. You can live for today and let your flesh have whatever it wants, or you can live for eternity and instead choose a life of purity. The choices are yours. But make no mistake about it: The choices of today will determine the outcome of your future. Choices that are based on the Lord and His ways lead to life and freedom. Choices made based on your will, your flesh, or the world will lead to bondage and ultimately death. As I look back on my own life, I feel so grateful that there were those who encouraged me to make the choice to forsake the world and follow God. For me that meant making a choice to walk away from a life of drugs, promiscuity, and violence and to turn toward the things of Christ. In the same way, I come to you today and encourage you to forsake the world and choose to wholeheartedly follow the Lord. Choose God. Choose life!

You may think that God just wants to cramp your style or that He does not understand if you want to "have a little fun." But realize that our omnipotent God, in His infinite wisdom and love, knows the truth: that choosing to pursue and serve Him will bring about *true* joy, peace, and goodness in your life. The alternative—choosing the world and its pleasures—in the end, is not fun. Even though sin may bring pleasure for a season, believe me, the consequence can be a lifetime of pain, despondency, and failure.

Dear reader, you *must* choose this day *whom* you will serve. Just as I came face-to-face with that decision more than 35 years ago, you too must make a choice. Fortunately for me, I made the greatest choice of my life. I chose to surrender all and follow Christ. Don't put off this decision until tomorrow or next year. You do not know what tomorrow holds in store for you. Why wait to find true pleasure, true joy, and true peace? Today is your day of decision. Today is the right time to commit your life to the Lord and get serious about following Him. Now is the time to get off the fence. Don't be fooled; everybody serves somebody or something. I guarantee that if you determine in your heart to serve God and you live to please Him, you will never regret that decision because He alone is deserving of your devotion.

Part I

DESERVING OF DEVOTION

Chapter 1

DESERVING OF DEVOTION

Would you devote yourself to someone you don't know? I doubt it, and if you did, I would likely question your motives!

Consider this: God has chosen you. He is devoted to you! In fact, He can't take His eyes off you. Why? Because He loves you. He loves you with a love that passes knowledge (Ephesians 3:19), and He is thinking about you every moment of every day.

The Bible says that His thoughts for you are more frequent than the quantity of all the sand particles of the sea throughout the world (Psalm 139:17-18). Consider this awesome thought for a moment. This is the God who measures the ocean waters in the palms of His hands. The earth is His footstool, and the heavens cannot contain Him. Yet this same Creator God—who made you—has chosen to think continually about you!

Just as He's chosen to be devoted to you, He likewise wants your devotion in return. This will only happen as you get to know Him. He wants a vibrant relationship with you—one that is filled with commitment, fellowship, and close communion.

Joshua, the Old Testament leader who led Israel into the Promised Land, understood this principle. The Bible describes Joshua as a man of integrity and humility and a *servant* of God. Early on in his life, Joshua had chosen to fully follow the Lord. There is no doubt he knew the Lord and had a close relationship with Him. As a matter of fact, in the book of Joshua, the Bible declares that Joshua had to actually remind the leaders of Israel of *everything* that God had done for the people. Joshua stood firmly on his choice to put God first, and therefore, he never wavered between two masters.

Joshua knew that God was deserving of his devotion. He had witnessed God's work in his life and in the lives of the Israelites for more than 80 years. Joshua saw how God miraculously brought the children of Israel out of Egypt; he witnessed the parting of the Red Sea; he watched God provide manna and water to His people while they wandered in the desert; he experienced God's Word fulfilled as the children of Israel stepped into the Promised Land; and he watched the walls of Jericho fall right before his very eyes as the priests did nothing more than obediently walk around the city walls.

At 110 years of age, Joshua told the leaders and people of Israel, "Now therefore, fear the LORD, serve Him in sincerity and in truth, and put away the gods which your fathers served on the other side of the River and in Egypt. Serve the

LORD! And if it seems evil to you to serve the LORD, choose for yourselves this day whom you will serve. . . . As for me and my house, we will serve the LORD" (Joshua 24:14-15).

Joshua gave the people of Israel an ultimatum. The Israelites were beginning to drift away—torn between two different masters. The people wanted God on their own terms. Yet Joshua said, "You can't have it both ways. You must make a choice." I've lived long enough to realize that everybody serves somebody or something. You either determine in your heart to serve God and live to please Him, or you choose the world and live to please yourself. There's no way to do both, even though in Joshua's day they tried. They were caught up in idolatry—worshiping other gods. At the same time, they also continued to worship the Lord God at the Tabernacle and to perform their religious rituals. Joshua confronted their idolatry and said that they could no longer continue to serve two masters. He reminded them of all that God had done for them and why He was worthy of their wholehearted devotion. However, the decision was theirs, and Joshua declared emphatically that no matter what they chose, he and his family were going to serve the Lord.

A GREAT GOD

Getting to know God means understanding the greatness of God and realizing all He has done for you. I believe that once you grasp these things, a deep thankfulness will move you to devote all of your heart to Him.

Joshua understood the greatness of God. He was deeply thankful, and he did not hesitate to serve God. He saw the Lord work in his life and knew God was worthy of his complete devotion. What about you? Have you personally seen or experienced the greatness of God? Are you thankfully serving Him? Have you made the declaration that He is deserving of your devotion?

In his exhortation to the Israelites (Joshua 24), Joshua reminded them of their great and awesome God. The principle laid out to the children of Israel back then still applies to each of us today. Truly understanding who God is and what God does for His people makes it easy to love Him in return and be devoted to Him. The apostle John said, "We love Him because He first loved us" (1 John 4:19).

I personally like how the apostle Paul said that "the goodness of God leads you to repentance" (Romans 2:4). For years I have thought about this verse and tried to clearly understand the depth of its meaning. Then one day, as I looked at my own life and God's great work to bring me to Him, it was as if a lightbulb clicked on and I finally understood it. Suddenly my mind was flooded with thoughts of all God had done for me. I knew without a doubt that it was His goodness that had turned me from a life of destruction to a life of devotion to Him.

When I lived with an outlaw motorcycle gang, destruction governed me. I ran with violent gang members, and many of my mornings began with the barrel of a gun in my face (talk about waking up on the wrong side of the bed!). Guns, drugs, and violence were all part of my lifestyle. My heart was filled with rage. My mind was bent on revenge. As much as I hate to admit it, I once chased my mom down the street with a machete in hand. Thankfully she was able to outrun me! My life was out of control, and inwardly I was desperate for help.

Eventually my bad choices led to a life of living in fear and poverty. I made my bed in the streets and didn't bathe for six months. Yet somehow God got ahold of my life, and through a variety of circumstances, He led me to Calvary Chapel Costa Mesa. It was there that I heard about a great God who loved me and died to prove His love for me. Pastor Chuck Smith welcomed me and assured me that Jesus accepted me just as I was. It was all I needed to hear. At that moment I realized I had a choice to make. I could choose to love God and serve Him in return, or I could continue down the path of destruction and leave God totally out of my life. Because no one had ever loved and accepted me like Jesus, the only choice for me was to give my life to Him. Since that day, I have devoted myself to loving and serving our great God and Savior, Jesus Christ.

After giving my heart to Jesus, He blessed me with a beautiful wife and two children. Exceeding every expectation, He also blessed me with an opportunity to serve Him as a pastor. Despite all I had done and all I had once been, I knew that God loved me. I knew it was His kindness that had drawn me to Him and His grace that had kept me every step of the way.

God is so deserving of your devotion. Don't hesitate to stop and reflect on your past. No matter what bad choices you have made, His great love causes Him to overlook these choices and extend His open arms to receive you. What He's done for me, He will do for you too. His goodness has always been toward His people. He is a great God willing to do great things for you—and for all of us. Joshua reminds Israel of this fact in Joshua 24:1-13. Take a moment to read these verses for yourself. In this passage he makes it clear that Yahweh is a great and awesome God who has blessed His people. He lays out four points for them to consider regarding their great God:

1. God *chose* Israel—and opened their hearts.
2. God *delivered* Israel—and opened the Sea.
3. God *guided* Israel—and opened the path.
4. God *blessed* Israel—and opened the Jordan.

Although thousands of years have passed since this truth was proclaimed, the same message applies today and is just as powerful. Like Israel, God *chose* you too. Long before you even knew Him, He loved you and wanted you. Just as He opened the Red Sea and delivered the Israelites from destruction, God has also opened up the way and *delivered* you. Rest assured, He will never forsake you when you call out to Him for help. As certainly as God guided Israel, so has He *guided* you and will continue to guide you through every wilderness experience into a better and more fruitful place. Finally, just as God blessed His children Israel, He will *bless* you, both now and in the future. There's no doubt that you have a great God who wants to do great and awesome things in your life! He loves you and will do anything for you— even give His only Son to die for you. Doesn't He deserve your devotion? What will your choice be?

Chapter 2

GOD CHOOSES YOU

Talk about an amazing choice—God choosing you and me. It's one thing for us to choose Him, but it's an entirely different thing to think that Almighty God has chosen us. But He has. And Joshua reminds the Israelites of this fact. He points out to them how God chose Abraham even when he was in a foreign country, was worshiping a foreign god, and had no knowledge of the Lord: "Then I took your father Abraham from the other side of the River, led him throughout all the land of Canaan, and multiplied his descendants and gave him Isaac" (Joshua 24:3).

The story that Joshua shared reminded the people of Israel that God chose them even as He had chosen Abraham. Abraham was lost in idolatry, yet the God of Glory appeared to him. God opened Abraham's heart to receive, bringing him out of darkness and into the light. God called Abraham out of Ur of Chaldeans, setting him apart with a plan and a purpose.

It is amazing that your Heavenly Father would reach down to you and say, "My son or daughter—*this is your day!*

Today I choose you. I want to stop you in the way you are going. Currently you are doomed in your sins, *but* I want to make you alive in Christ Jesus. I want to save you by My mighty grace and start you down the right path that I have ordained for your life—that onward and upward call."

Sound impossible? Well, it's not. This is exactly what happened to the apostle Paul. The Bible says that he was apprehended by God. This word *apprehended* means to be arrested, held, or overtaken. The Spirit of Christ overtook Paul right there on the Damascus Road (see Acts 9). On that very day, God chose Paul and turned his life around forever. To the man who was once called Saul of Tarsus, it was just another ordinary day, but to God it was the day Saul (later renamed Paul) was to be apprehended and transformed into a servant of the Most High God. It was the day God's Spirit would set Paul on the right course, making the right choices for the kingdom of God.

Likewise, the call of God came to Abraham on an ordinary day. What Abraham was doing that day was no different than what he had done any other previous day. *But this day was Abraham's day*—the day God chose him and the day that would forever change his life. *God chose him,* and Abraham could not add one thing to his salvation or calling. The same is true for you: God chooses you, and you are simply left with the choice of how you will respond.

Let me remind you, God reached down and chose Abraham to serve Him even when Abraham was in rebellion toward God. In the same way, God chose you before you had any knowledge of His existence. It is God who speaks to you and calls you to Himself. It is the Lord who takes you out of your sinful life and brings you into His kingdom. Quite frankly, there is nothing you can do to choose God without Him first choosing you. Does that mean that some people do not go to heaven because God did not choose them? No. The Bible clearly states that God desires for no man to perish. He has given every person a free will. With that free will comes the power to choose. Each man or woman can choose to obey or choose to disobey. His call is upon each of us. So, God chooses you, but you have the choice to refuse to respond to His offer. God called Paul out of his prideful, self-centered, destructive lifestyle, and Paul responded. God called Abraham out of idolatry, and Abraham obeyed. Paul's choice led him to be the greatest and most influential disciple ever known. Abraham's choice led him to be called a friend of God's and to be entrusted as the father of a nation of people whom God called His very own.

In the same way, God is calling you to choose to follow Him. He wants to open your heart and bring you from darkness into His marvelous light. He wants to lead you out of the world and into His purpose and plan for your life. This has been His plan for you from before the foundation of the world. No wonder the apostle Paul said, "Blessed be the God and Father of our Lord Jesus Christ, who has blessed us with every spiritual blessing in the heavenly places in Christ, *just as He chose us in Him before the foundation of the world,* that we should be holy and without blame before Him in love, *having predestined us to adoption as sons by Jesus Christ to Himself,* according to the good pleasure of His will" (Ephesians 1:3-5, emphasis added).

You have been chosen! God chose you. You don't find Jesus. He finds you. The late great preacher Dr. Harry A. Ironside told this story:

> A little boy was asked, "Have you found Jesus?" The little fellow answered, "Sir, I didn't know He was lost. But I was lost and He found me."

Each of us is in exactly the same condition as that little boy—lost. Fortunately for all of us, Jesus is on a search. He is looking for those who are lost and want to be rescued. I'll never forget the pictures engraved in my mind of the people who were affected by that disastrous tsunami in late December of 2004. People were literally holding on with all their might to a tree trunk, house top, or floating piece of debris, waiting to be rescued. Desperately they waited to be pulled from death and disaster. I can't imagine the overwhelming relief they must have felt when help finally came. The same scenario is true for all people who are spiritually lost. They are caught in the middle of a disastrous and fallen world. They've been swooped up in the current of worldliness. The tide of sin is overtaking them. There's no way out unless they are rescued. God knew that. That's why He sent

Jesus. But they have to *want* to be rescued. The victims of the tsunami didn't waive away help hoping for a "better" or "different" way out—no way. They were desperate! They knew genuine help had arrived, and they just grabbed hold of the lifeline and their lives were spared. That's what Jesus wants to do for the lost.

In the Bible, He is the One who went out after the lost sheep. He is the One who found that sheep, and He is the One who rejoices with exceeding joy when that sheep is rescued. You and I represent that lost sheep. Because of God's amazing grace, I was found more than 35 years ago, and my life has never been the same. Jesus reached out His hand to rescue me, and I took hold and have never let go! Let me ask you this: Has Jesus found His way into your heart?

God chose believers in Christ before the foundation of the world, way back in eternity past. That means we didn't do the choosing; God did. But never forget that He did not choose us because we were good or because we would do some good. He chose us because He saw our desperate need to be rescued. I can fully relate to what Charles Spurgeon once said, "God chose me before I came into the world, because if He'd waited until I got here, He never would have chosen me." Thankfully, God chooses us based on His great love and not on our good works.

God has chosen you, but you have to respond! Are you desperate enough? It's up to you whether you'll accept His free gift of salvation or not. It's up to you whether you'll accept the lifeline He's thrown out to you. The choice is yours. But I guarantee that once you make the choice, He'll be waiting right there with open arms to rescue and deliver you!

Chapter 3

GOD DELIVERS YOU

Not only did Joshua want the people of Israel to know that God had chosen them, he also wanted them to fully understand that it was the Lord God who delivered them from their enemies and brought them out of bondage—out of the land of Egypt. Joshua told them the words of the Lord: "Also I sent Moses and Aaron, and I plagued Egypt, according to what I did among them. Afterward I brought you out" (Joshua 24:5).

This verse reminds us that only the Lord can turn evil into good. Look at the life of Joseph. He was the favored son of Jacob, betrayed by his jealous brothers and sold into slavery in Egypt. However, God sent Joseph into Egypt to fulfill His greater purpose and turned his desperation of poverty into a destination of provisions from God. Similarly, no matter what happens to you, God chooses to deliver you if you will cooperate with Him. Joseph himself said to his brothers, "You meant evil against me; but God meant it for good" (Genesis 50:20). God had to get Joseph into Egypt so He could reveal His mighty plan of redemption throughout the world. God delivered Israel through Joseph. Your reaction might be, "That isn't fair! Why would Joseph have to suffer and go through so much pain?

"A. W. Tozer had an interesting thought that may shed some light on this question: "It is doubtful if God could ever use a man greatly, *until* He hurts that man deeply."

What great insight that is. Tozer understood and saw the wisdom of how God makes and molds His men and women. It is right here that many of us lose out. We choose to question God's love and oftentimes turn away in bitterness, blaming God for everything.

Martha, a friend of Jesus in the New Testament, is a classic example of this. Seeing Jesus returning to her hometown, she ran to Him and said, "If You had been here, my brother would not have died" (John 11:21). In essence she was saying, "My brother is dead because You took Your time getting here." Jesus understood her grief, but at the same time He explained that her brother's death occurred for the glory of God. Martha just couldn't see things from the divine perspective so she blamed God. It would sure make life easier. Sometimes if we could see things from God's perspective. Yet testing and trials have a way of breaking us and molding us into His image. Therefore, determine right now that you will make the choice to trust God and give Him the opportunity to deliver you before you go through something that hurts you deeply. If you'll do this, I can assure you that He will turn your pain into gain. Like Tozer suggested, you'll be ready for God to use you greatly!

Years after Joseph, God sent Moses into Egypt to intervene and help His people—the Israelites. Through Moses, God sent the plagues so that the children of Israel would be freed from Pharaoh's bondage and sent out to the Promised Land. On the Israelites' way out of Egypt, God opened the Red Sea to separate the people from Egypt.

What is the message? *God delivers!*

In the Bible, Egypt is equivalent to the secular world with its enticements, immorality, and wrong values. When the Israelites were in Egypt, they unfortunately began to act like the Egyptians.

Because of this, the Egyptians enslaved the children of Israel. As the children of Israel multiplied, the bondage intensified with hardship and oppression. That's the way sin works. It starts out as a simple temptation—a seemingly harmless flirtation—but then accelerates to a way of life and finally ensnares you. Sin is nothing short of bondage. It always takes you further than you ever intended to go. It always costs you more than you ever wanted to pay. You may have enjoyed the sin in the beginning (remember, the Bible states that sin is pleasurable for a season), but eventually you find that your bondage is far from anything good or pleasurable.

The apostle James said in his epistle, "When desire has conceived, it gives birth to sin; and sin, when it is full-grown, brings forth death" (James 1:15). In other words, sin will never lead to anything good. That's why you need to be delivered.

If you feel trapped with no way out—you are in bondage. If you have tried time and again to stop your habitual sin but can't—you are in bondage.

It is possible to become so trapped in sin that all vision for what is right is lost. Remember Samson, the judge of Israel? His detailed story is found in chapter 16 of the Old Testament book of Judges. Here we find God's man bound to a grinding wheel, blinded by the Philistines and grinding around and around and in desperate need of deliverance! How did he ever get there? It was his foolish choices and unfaithfulness to God that landed him in this horrible mess. At some point Samson had lost the fear of God in his life; he began to believe in himself and his strength instead of God's miraculous supernatural power at work in him. He felt no one could touch him. But Samson had failed to take into consideration that it was God who had given him this special power and might and that it was God who would allow it to be taken away. You see, Samson was no longer willing to listen or repent, and therefore, his choices ultimately led the Philistines to defeat and dishonor him.

Sometimes, like the Egyptians, we become so involved with the world that we make terrible decisions that lead us into bondage. Sometimes, like Samson, we get prideful and flirt with sin and then our choices lead us right into the hands of the enemy. Bad choices draw us closer and closer to destruction. The only way to break this path of ruin is to make the choice to turn away from sin and turn to Christ. Only Jesus can deliver us from the bondage of sin!

Just as God delivered the children of Israel from the bondage of Egypt, He wants to deliver you from the power of sin in your life. The very reason Jesus gave His life was so that He might deliver you from this present evil age (Galatians 1:4). Jesus Christ conquered your sin on the cross. He is able to change you and set you free from the sins that hold you in bondage. Is it any wonder that the Gospel is called the Good News? The question is: Do you believe this Good News? Jesus has delivered you! He has made the choice to be your Deliverer. Now you must make the choice to accept His help. I urge you, don't be like Samson and waste away your life before you finally surrender. You must choose today whom you will serve. Pause right now and turn your life completely over to Him. Through prayer, ask Him to deliver you out of anything that is holding you in bondage.

Now rejoice because not only can God deliver you, but the Scriptures promise that He is able to keep you from stumbling or slipping or falling and to present you blameless and faultless before the presence of His glory with unspeakable and ecstatic delight (Jude 24). God has so much in store for you if you choose to follow Him. Not only does Jesus deliver you, but He will guide you through this life and on into eternity to present you before the Father with great joy!

Chapter 4

GOD GUIDES YOU

God delivered Israel. With the enemy pressing in hard, the people stood at the edge of the Red Sea with seemingly nowhere to go. They cried out to God, and He miraculously opened the Red Sea and made a way out for them. With walls of water towering around them, He guided them through on dry land to the other side. Then He let these same walls collapse to cover their enemy. And He didn't stop with their deliverance. From there *God guided* them day by day.

Joshua reminded the people how God guided the children of Israel out of their bondage and into the Promised Land. He did just as He said He would. However, because of their disobedience, they had to wander in the desert for 40 years in order to learn a few vital lessons. Yet even in their disobedience, He continued to guide them. He fed them manna, gave them water from a rock, and protected them the entire time they were in the desert.

Joshua 24:7-8 describes God's personal involvement and guidance in the battles of His people: "Then you dwelt in the wilderness a long time. And I brought you into the land of the Amorites, who dwelt on the other side of the Jordan, and they fought with you. But I gave them into your hand, that you might possess their land, and I destroyed them from before you."

If the children of Israel had been obedient and followed the Lord closely, they would have made it to the Promised Land a lot earlier. Yet their bad choices led them to wander and struggle in the desert in a way God never intended. Technically, it only should have taken them a couple of weeks to get where they were going. However, because of their stubbornness and their persistence to worship other gods, they spent 40 years wandering in a desert experience. If I were God, I would have given up on them! But He didn't. He never does. That's why He's God and I'm not!

Maybe you feel like you're wandering in a desert as well. Your journeys feel far more strenuous, sorrowful, and shallow than you think they should be. Could it be that perhaps you too have been disobedient to God? And your disobedience is leading you to wander aimlessly in a way God never intended? Your choice to follow your own way instead of the Lord's always will lead you along a hard and costly path.

Disobedience is a refusal to obey. Once you disobey the Lord, the next step of disobedience is not so difficult. Before long you are walking out of His way and His will altogether. Wandering. Struggling. Lost and miserable. *Why obey God*, you think? First, understand that God requires it. Second,

God is a good Father who knows what is best for His children. His heart is to guide you, and your obedience will lead you to His very best for your life. Your obedience will lead you into His land of promises.

Joshua states that "nevertheless, He guided Israel." Through the wilderness, through the place of disobedience, through the place of murmuring, and through the place of fighting—to the Jordan and on into the Promised Land—He faithfully guided His people.

The phrase, "nevertheless, He guided Israel," is a great comfort. It should give you great hope concerning God's love for you and should encourage you that He is willing to work through all your shortcomings and wanderings. It is often easy to complain and murmur against His plans and purposes. Do you find this to occur in your life? Do you allow yourself to feel cheated, overlooked, or even left out, and then do just what the Israelites did—murmur and complain about the way God is leading you? Fortunately, the Bible emphatically states that He will never leave or forsake you. He willingly offers to you His hand and patiently guides you through every storm of life. He will be there for you even in your darkest hours. But once again, you must make the choice to follow His lead. You must take hold of His hand and let Him navigate you through this life.

Letting God lead and guide is a necessity. Consider the following story:

There was a young physician who was deter-mined to reach the heights of Mount Banc, the highest peak in Europe. When he made it to the top of the peak, the little village at the foot of the mountain was illuminated in his honor; on the mountainside, a flag was floating that told of his victory.

After he had ascended and descended as far as the hut, he wanted to be released from his guide; he wanted to be free from the rope and insisted on going alone.

The guide told him it was not safe; but the young physician was tired of the rope and declared that he would be free. The guide was compelled to yield. The young man had gone only a short dis-tance when his foot slipped on the ice, and he could not stop himself from sliding down the icy steps. The rope was gone, so the guide could not hold him or pull him back. Out on the shelving ice lay the body of the young physician.

The bells had been rung, and the village had been illuminated in honor of his success. But alas, in a fatal moment, he refused to be guided; he was tired of the rope.

God guided the children of Israel, but they, like the young physician, tired of His "rope." Even though He took care of their needs, miraculously delivered them from their enemies, and repeatedly communed with them and assured them of His plan for their lives, they wanted to direct their own path. Each time they took matters into their own hands, they were met with trouble and destruction.

Just for a moment, think about all the "circumstances" that have happened in your life that, at the time, you didn't understand. But later when you looked back over them, you could absolutely see His hand through it all.

I can remember many "circumstances" that happened in my life. For instance, in 1996 I went through so many illnesses that I was hospitalized four times and was out of the pulpit for six months. The following year, gang members murdered my son-in-law; one of my pastors, a chaplain with the sheriff's department, was shot and killed in the line of service; and the church was going through a building project. At times it felt like more than I could ever handle. But now as I look back over these events, I can clearly see that through it all God was with me and guiding me.

I see how God allowed the instrument of sickness and painful circumstances to work in and through my life. He allowed me to go through those times because He wanted to change me. He had a plan and a purpose to use me in a new and greater work in my ministry at Calvary Chapel South Bay and in the Los Angeles area. Yet before He could do this, there was work to be done on my heart. He wasn't interested in making me comfortable; He was in the process of making me a comforter. Just as He had guided me through these times of heartache, He wanted me in turn to guide others.

I wish I could say that I went through all of this without once letting go of His rope. Unfortunately, there were times when I did take matters into my own hands. Maybe you've done this too. Maybe you're in a place today in which you're considering letting go. Could it be that you've taken your eyes off of the Lord and placed them on someone or something else thinking that's the answer? Maybe you've just lost hope. Be careful. Disappointment, self-confidence, pride . . . all of these things will tempt you into a bad choice. Before you know it, you'll let go of His rope and be headed for a disaster. Trust me—it's time to grab hold of that rope. Better yet, it's time to let Him tie you up in His rope of love.

God guides His people's lives. Joshua knew it. The Israelites knew it. I know it, and now you know it too. He alone knows what's best, and His path always leads to your ultimate peace and joy. If you are His child, He is guiding and leading you right now. If you're in the midst of painful circumstances, hold on and let Him change your heart through it all. The God of heaven has your life in His capable hands. He will not steer you in the wrong direction. So don't let go of Him. You may not know where He's taking you, but you can know that He has your best interest in mind.

Martin Luther once said, "I know not the way He leads me, but *well* do I know *my* Guide." Let me ask you: How well do you know your Guide? How familiar are you with the Lord and His promises? Read the Word of God daily so you can get to know Him well. His Word will help you not to lose your grip as you go through life. I promise you that your Guide—the Lord Jesus Christ—will not disappoint you. Choose to hold fast to Him and follow wherever He leads. This is the only way to have a future that's bright and promising and full of His blessings!

Chapter 5

GOD BLESSES YOU

Finally, Joshua reminded the children of Israel that it was God who *blessed* them. God had the battle plan; He brought them out of Jericho; He destroyed their enemies, and He gave them the Promised Land. In God's own words, He said, "I have given you a land for which you did not labor, and cities which you did not build, and you dwell in them; you eat of the vineyards and olive groves which you did not plant" (Joshua 24:13).

God blessed the children of Israel in spite of themselves! In spite of all their bad choices, He gave them things that they did not earn. Why? Because God loves and is committed to His people. The apostle Paul said, "If we are faithless, He remains faithful; He cannot deny Himself" (2 Timothy 2:13). God is faithful to you even when you are not faithful to Him! And He blesses your life—sometimes when you *least* deserve it.

No doubt the apostle Peter experienced this when he failed God. Do you remember Peter's denial of the Lord? Hours before the crucifixion, Peter is found at the enemy's camp, warming himself at their fire. (Note the spiritual connotations of that: When you are not faithful to the Lord, the result is a downward spiral of spiritual regression in your heart. Before you know it, you are trying to find contentment with carnality and the company of the world rather than Christ.) As is often the case, one bad decision leads to another. Next, Peter makes the choice to deny knowing the Lord. He does this two more times and even curses the Lord. Nevertheless, at that very moment, the Lord looks at Peter with compassionate eyes. Peter was sorrowful beyond words. Yet on resurrection day, guess who purposed to find and restore Peter? The Lord! To top it all off, guess who was used to preach the very first message to thousands after the Lord's ascension? Peter! God is definitely good to us, in spite of ourselves.

You're no different from Peter. God chooses to bless you in many ways! It's not as if He's forced to bless you; rather, it's His very nature. He freely chooses to pour out His abundant goodness, and without restraint or hesitation He does so. Just as Peter and the Israelites were recipients of God's blessings, so are you. Let me share with you just a couple of the many ways you are blessed.

First, God blesses you through His eternal plans. Set in His heart and mind from the very beginning of time, God wanted to bless Abraham. He had a plan that would bless not only Abraham but also his family and all the families of the earth. You are part of that blessing. Genesis 12:3 says, "I will bless those who bless you, and I will curse him who curses you; and in you all the families of the earth shall be blessed." God called Abraham out of a godless, self-centered life. God promised to bless Abraham and make him great, but Abraham had to do what God wanted him to do. He left his home and friends and traveled to a new land where God promised to build a great nation from Abraham's family!

God may be trying to lead you to a place of greater service and usefulness for Him. Don't let the comfort and security of your present position make you miss God's plan for you. He wants to bless your life. But it all begins with your choice to obey. Like Abraham, once you obediently say "yes" to God, He begins to move you in the direction of His eternal plans for your life and to pour out His blessings.

Second, God blesses you through His Son Jesus. In fact, Jesus is God's greatest blessing of all. Ephesians 1:3 (NLT) says, "How we praise God, the Father of our Lord Jesus Christ, who has blessed us with every spiritual blessing in the heavenly realms because we belong to Christ."

As a believer in Christ, you have *all* benefits. Paul explains in Ephesians 1 that you are blessed because of God and because you belong to Christ. You have been *chosen* for salvation, *predestined* for life, *adopted* as His child, *accepted* by a loving Savior, *redeemed* by His blood, *forgiven* of your sins, and *given insight* through His Word. You have *obtained an eternal inheritance* and are *sealed* by the Holy Spirit. And finally, you are *assured* of the power to do God's will and have the hope of living forever with Christ. Now that's quite a list of blessings! Won't you agree, with all that being said, *you* could do *nothing else* but choose to love and serve God? When you choose Christ and commit your heart and life to Him, the floodgate of blessing from above is opened and you are filled to overflow with His benefits.

Furthermore, if you have an intimate relationship with Christ, you can begin enjoying these blessings now. "In the heavenly realms" means that these blessings are eternal, not temporal.

Making good and godly choices begins with an understanding that God made choices first. He's not asking you to do something He's never done. His first and most significant choice was when He chose you. Yes, *God chooses you*. That very choice led Him to sacrifice His only Son to prove His choice was real. From there *God delivers you, God guides you,* and *God blesses you*—these are all more than enough reasons for why God is deserving of your devotion! Now you have to make a choice; we might call it your "day of decision." God has made His choice obvious and clear. He loves you. He's devoted to you. And now He's waiting to know: What will your choice be? Whom will you serve?

Part II

DAY OF DECISION

Chapter 6

DAY OF DECISION

No one can escape making a decision for or against Christ. Someone once said, "When you have to make a decision and don't make it, that is in of itself a decision." Perhaps that's why Jesus said, "No one can serve two masters; for either he will hate the one and love the other, or else he will be loyal to the one and despise the other. You cannot serve God and mammon [treasures]" (Matthew 6:24).

To ignore your day of decision simply means that you have decided to live independent of Christ. To avoid this decision by trying to live with one foot in the world and one foot in Christ is impossible, not to mention that it will have disastrous consequences.

In the Old Testament, King Saul, the first king of Israel, is a perfect example of someone who tried to serve two masters. He did what God told him, *but* he did it *his* way. Even though he wanted God, he could not let go of his own independent will. Thus in the end, he really didn't follow God at all. Eventually this lifestyle cost him his kingdom and his life.

The Bible tells us how God gave Saul blessings upon blessings. Yet in spite of all these wonderful things, King Saul chose to rebel. It was after many occasions of choosing to disobey God that He gave Saul one more chance to make the right choice. God gave Saul an ultimatum and literally brought him to his day of decision. God told him specifically, "I want you to utterly destroy the Amalekites and all living things from their land" (see 1 Samuel 15:3). Saul then goes to battle and is victorious, yet he returns from the battle in total disobedience. The prophet Samuel, now blind by his age, greets him on his return and says, "What is that I hear with you? It sounds like sheep, and who else is with you, standing before me?" Saul told Samuel, "I brought the sheep back to sacrifice, and this is the king of the Amalekites." Not good. God said to bring back nothing—not the sheep, not the king, nothing! Yet Saul chose to do just the opposite.

So, Saul made his decision when he refused to wholly obey God. Because of this, Samuel then has to finish the job. He takes a sword and kills the Amalekite king; then he turns to King Saul and prophetically declares, "Your kingdom shall be taken and given to another." Samuel then speaks one of the most powerful passages in the Bible to this foolish king before he walks away from him:

> So Samuel said: "Has the LORD as great delight in burnt offerings and sacrifices, as in obeying the voice of the LORD? Behold, to obey is better than

sacrifice, and to heed than the fat of rams. For rebellion is as the sin of witchcraft, and stubbornness is as iniquity and idolatry. Because you have rejected the word of the LORD, He also has rejected you from being king."

Then Saul said to Samuel, "I have sinned, for I have transgressed the commandment of the LORD and your words, because I feared the people and obeyed their voice. Now therefore, please pardon my sin, and return with me, that I may worship the LORD."

But Samuel said to Saul, "I will not return with you, for you have rejected the word of the Lord, and the Lord has rejected you from being king over Israel."

And as Samuel turned around to go away, Saul seized the edge of his robe, and it tore. So Samuel said to him, "The LORD has torn the kingdom of Israel from you today, and has given it to a neighbor of yours, who is better than you" (1 Samuel 15:22-28).

Saul made foolish and selfish choices and subsequently lost his kingdom. What is even more interesting in this story of King Saul is how his own life ends. Remember how he was commanded to destroy *all* of the Amalekites? Well, during his last battle he was wounded. Fearful of falling into the hands of the enemy, he looks for someone to kill him. Saul saw a young man nearby and begged him to kill him. Before this young man kills him, Saul asks, "Who are you?" The young man looks at him and says, "I am an Amalekite." Think about the irony: Saul was supposed to destroy all the Amalekites, and now it was an Amalekite who claimed to kill Saul (2 Samuel 1:7-10).

Sounds like us believers at times, doesn't it? In a similar way, God tells us to destroy and have nothing to do with the flesh, but instead we play with it and one day it comes back to harm us. Somehow we try to be "in Christ" and in the world at the same time. We foolishly try to place ourselves under two masters, and inevitably this decision leads to our destruction. We must clearly choose one master and then make our decisions based on that. We must choose to listen to God's Word, and when He speaks, we must wholly follow Him. Anything less is to live a selfish and foolish life.

At a personal level, consider your choices lately. What do they reflect? Do you find yourself knowing what is "right" to do yet doing differently? If others were evaluating your life, would they know whom you serve?

The Bible reflects many choices: two roads, two wills, two opinions, two masters, two gates, two standards, two gods. What choice will you make? In the book of Amos, the prophet declares, "Can two walk together, unless they are agreed?" (Amos 3:3). In other words, unless you agree with the Lord, you are not walking with Him!

Joshua reminded Israel that there is a day of decision in every life. Similarly for you, along with the choices you make come *consequences* and *confirmations.* The following chapters will reflect on and consider these same points that Joshua shared with the Israelites several thousand years ago:

1. The choices—It's time to choose.
2. The consequences—It's time to consider.
3. The confirmation—It's time to reaffirm.

Remember, you cannot give everything to God if your commitment is divided between the things of heaven and the things of the world. In fact, it's impossible. Worse yet, when your commitment and devotion are divided between two masters, you inevitably end up following the master of this world and those things that entice you away from the Lord. In the final outcome, you find yourself completely away from the Lord and absorbed in the life of the flesh.

Like Saul and like the Israelites, you eventually will come to a day of decision. Joshua's exhortation to "choose . . . this day whom you will serve" stands throughout all ages—you too must choose. I urge you to choose carefully. Choose prayerfully. Your choice will determine your future.

Chapter 7

THE CHOICES

If there's one thing I've seen more than anything else in my years as a pastor, it's the heartbreak of bad choices. As I counsel people and help them put their broken lives back together, I often try to take them back to the very place at which they first began making bad choices, the place at which they stopped listening to God. I want them to learn that if they're going to walk with the Lord, then they must learn to listen to what He says "to do" and "not to do." That's what Joshua reminds the Israelites. He lets them know that there will be choices they have to make, and these choices include the "things to do" and the "things not to do."

Consider the choices Joshua gave the people: "Now therefore, fear the LORD, serve Him in sincerity and in truth, and put away the gods which your fathers served on the other side of the River and in Egypt. Serve the LORD!" (Joshua 24:14).

Reverence, service, sincerity, truth, and purity are all choices God gives you strength to make. These were the things the Israelites were to do. It's as if Joshua said, "It is time to make a choice to awake out of your sleep. It's time to serve the Lord, to speak the truth, and to clean house."

In a similar way, the apostle Paul reminds us in his letter to the Ephesians, "Redeeming the time, because the days are evil" (Ephesians 5:16). In other words, we are to make every moment count. We are not to waste any of our days or hours here on earth. Literally we are to "buy back" everything lost—for the glory of God.

What about you? What choices are you making today? Are you making every moment count? Are you awake? Are you serving the Lord? Are you speaking the truth? And are you allowing your life to be cleansed?

Joshua then makes it clear that there are the "things not to do." Don't go backward. Don't serve the gods of this world! This is what he says: "And if it seems evil to you to serve the LORD, choose for yourselves this day whom you will serve, whether the gods which your fathers served that were on the other side of the River, or the gods of the Amorites, in whose land you dwell" (Joshua 24:15).

Simply put, here are your two choices: Either serve the true and living God (the LORD), or you will serve the gods of this world. Quite frankly, it is easy to see what choice you have made by observing your lifestyle. Furthermore, the choice you make will always be followed by commitment.

President Eisenhower understood this. He readily admitted that public speaking was not his forte but that he was obviously committed to public speaking as president of the

United States. Addressing an audience one day, he told the following story:

> A neighboring farmer had a cow that he wanted to sell. We went over to visit the farmer and asked him about the cow's pedigree. The old farmer didn't know what *pedigree* meant, so we asked him about the cow's butterfat production. He told us he didn't have any idea what it was. Finally, we asked him if he knew how many pounds of milk the cow produced each year. The farmer said, "I don't know. But she's an honest cow, and she'll give you all the milk she has."

Eisenhower then said, "I'm like that cow. I'll give you everything I have."

What a simple yet pointed illustration of commitment. Someone once said, "There's a difference between interest and commitment. When you're interested in doing something, you do it only when it's convenient. When you're committed to something, you accept no excuses, only results." Eisenhower's commitment caused him to do everything he could—even things outside his comfort zone. He wasn't just interested in being a good president; he was committed to it, and his choices proved this. How committed are you as a Christian? It's not enough to be just interested in Christ. You must make a commitment to Him. And that commitment involves several things. Let's consider, for a moment, your commitment to God and what it entails.

Your commitment to Christ begins with trust.

> Psalm 37:5 (NLT) says, "Commit everything you do to the LORD. Trust him, and he will help you."

> David the psalmist calls you to trust in the Lord and to commit everything you have and do to Him. But how do you do this? Simply put, you do it one choice at a time.

> Committing everything to the Lord means entrusting your life, family, job, and possessions to His control and guidance. To commit yourself to the Lord means trusting in Him, believing that He can care for you better than you can care for yourself. The opposite of trust is doubt, and if you doubt the Lord and His Word, then you will have a difficult time choosing to obey Him. Let me tell you from years of walking with the Lord—He is worthy to be trusted! The more you get to know Him, the easier this trust will come. Then as you trust Him, you'll learn to wait patiently for Him to work out what is best for you!

Your commitment to Christ must be complete.

Jesus said, "Follow me now! Let those who are spiritually dead care for their own dead" (Matthew 8:22, NLT).

Jesus was speaking to a disciple about this man's desire to follow Him at a later time. It's possible that this disciple was asking permission to put off following Jesus until his elderly father died. Or maybe he was the firstborn son and wanted to be sure to claim his inheritance before he made a complete commitment to follow Christ. He may even have been afraid of his father's wrath if he left the family business to follow a traveling preacher. Whether his concern was financial security, family approval, or something else, it's evident that he did not want to fully commit himself to Jesus just yet. However, Jesus was not satisfied with this type of partial and halfhearted commitment. He was looking for complete devotion.

Jesus was always direct with those who wanted to follow Him. He made sure they counted the cost and set aside any conditions they might have for following Him. Following God demands complete loyalty. Nothing should be placed above a total commitment to living for Him.

Jesus said to those who wanted to follow Him, "Foxes have holes and birds of the air have nests, but the Son of Man has nowhere to lay His head" (Matthew 8:20). The allegory is simple. Jesus was saying it is best to count the cost. When you personally come to your day of decision, it will require you to make a complete and wholehearted decision for Christ. Anything less will cause you to waiver in your commitment and be inconsistent in your choices.

Your commitment to Christ must be consistent.

Joshua said, "If you are unwilling to serve the LORD, then choose today whom you will serve. Would you prefer the gods your ancestors served beyond the Euphrates [who worshiped idols]? Or will it be the gods of the Amorites [who worshiped pleasure] in whose land you now live? But as for me and my family, we will serve the LORD" (Joshua 24:15, NLT).

The people had to decide whether they would obey the Lord, who had proven trustworthy, or obey the local gods, which were no more than man-made idols. Joshua made his decision. Without wavering, without inconsistency, he stood and declared that he and his family would serve only the Lord.

It's easy to slip into a quiet rebellion by just going about life in your own way. But the time comes when you must choose who or what will control you. Joshua took a definite stand for the Lord. Regardless of what others were doing, Joshua made a commitment to the Lord and was willing to consistently live out that decision.

In the same way, your commitment to the Lord must be consistent. He is worthy of your devotion, and it can't be shared with other gods in your life!

Will you choose to *trust* Christ? Will you wholeheartedly and unreservedly give Him your *complete* and *consistent* devotion? If so, then your life, like Joshua's, will be rich and full and most of all pleasing to the Lord.

Chapter 8

THE CONSEQUENCES

I recently came across an illustration that really emphasized the importance of making good choices. When you continually make poor choices in life, you set yourself up to have a bad reputation. A bad reputation inevitably leads to consequences that are not easy to face. Consider this humorous but telling story.

> Two young boys, Andy and Jim, were excessively mischievous. The two were always getting into trouble, and their parents could be sure that if any mischief occurred in their town, their two sons were probably involved in some way.
>
> One day, the mother heard that there was a clergyman in town who had been successful in disciplining children. She asked her husband if he thought they should send the boys to speak with the clergyman. The husband said, "We might as well. Nothing else is working."

The clergyman agreed to speak with the boys, but he asked to see them individually. The eight-year-old went to meet with him first. The clergyman sat the boy down and asked him sternly, "Where is God?" The boy made no response. The clergyman repeated the question in an even sterner tone: "Where is God?" Again, the boy made no attempt to answer. The clergyman raised his voice even more and shook his finger in the boy's face: "Where is God?"

With that, the boy bolted from the room and ran directly home, slamming his door and hiding himself in his closet. His older brother followed him into the closet and said, "What happened?" The younger brother replied, "We are in big trouble this time! GOD IS MISSING AND THEY THINK WE DID IT!"

As humorous as this story is, we can see that these mischievous boys obviously were reaping what they had sowed. The moral is clear: Be careful what seeds you sow because there will be consequences! Consider your own life for a moment. Are you sowing seeds of sin or seeds of righteousness? What are you known for? What kind of reputation follows you? Make no mistake about it—when you make bad choices that lead you to sow seeds of compromise, idolatry, and carnality, you will reap a foolish, futile, and failing life.

Joshua reminds the people that it's time to consider that there will be consequences for bad choices. He warns them that if for some reason they ever choose to forsake God, they will reap the consequences of this decision: "*If* you forsake the LORD and serve other gods, [*then*] he will turn against you and destroy you, even though he has been so good to you" (Joshua 24:20, NLT, emphasis added).

In other words, *if* you turn your back on the Lord and walk away from Him, the path you choose for yourself will become a path of destruction, pain, and agony. This principle of life cannot be escaped: You reap what you sow.

Hosea the prophet emphasizes this same warning. He basically tells the people that there is a "cause" and "effect" for their choices: "If you sow the wind, you will reap the whirlwind" (see Hosea 8:7). How crucial then to understand that each seed you sow, each deed you do, and every word you speak will affect your life and the lives of others.

Don't be fooled. Every choice you make in life makes a statement about you. Your choices reflect that either you are a child of God or you are contrary to Him and His message. Jesus put it this way in Matthew's Gospel: "He who is not with Me is against Me, and he who does not gather with Me scatters abroad" (Matthew 12:30). Are you standing with Jesus in your choices? Does there seem to be a whirlwind surrounding your life—one bad thing after another happening faster than you can take it? Consider that this may be a result of the choices you've made—seeds you've sown. Ultimately, bad choices lead you in a downward spiral.

In the book of Romans regarding the downward spiral of bad choices, the apostle Paul said, "For although they knew God, they neither glorified him as God nor gave thanks to him, *but* their thinking became futile and their foolish hearts were darkened. Although they claimed to be wise, they became fools. . . . Therefore God gave them over in the sinful desires of their hearts to sexual impurity for the degrading of their bodies with one another. They exchanged the truth of God for a lie, and worshiped and served created things rather than the Creator" (Romans 1:21-25, NIV, emphasis added).

Make no mistake about it. When you sow the wind, you reap the whirlwind. When you sow sin after sin, you eventually do or say things you never imagined! In the end, you, too, will foolishly exchange the truth of God for a lie. There are no excuses. You can only blame yourself for your decisions. As a young man, I made one bad decision after another. Eventually my life was no more than a whirlwind. I was on drugs, lonely, and living in the streets. I had lost my family, my friends, my job—everything. Fortunately for me, it was at this place that I found the Lord. Had it not been for that, I doubt that I would even be alive today. Worse yet, my downward spiral would have literally led me to hell. Always keep in mind that when you sow a thought, you reap an action; then when you sow an action, you reap a habit; and ultimately when you sow a habit, you will reap your destiny!

Let us now look at three areas of sin—compromise, idolatry, and carnality—the sowing of which will reap terrible consequences.

THE PROBLEM WITH COMPROMISE

The problem with compromise is that it has a way of looking enticing and innocent, but in the end it leads you into destruction. When believers start compromising in the area of sin, they reap a whirlwind of disaster. Once the compromise begins, it leads to a further regression of full-blown sin, which, in turn, leads to a lifestyle of sin and a departure from following the Lord.

What am I saying? Never compromise! Compromise only leads you into one problem after another. What are the problems associated with compromise? Let's take a look at just a few.

Compromise is the first step toward disobedience.

> First Kings 11:4 (NIV) says, "As Solomon grew old, his wives turned his heart after other gods, and his heart was not fully devoted to the Lord his God, as the heart of David his father had been."

> Solomon was pressured by his wives to worship other gods. At first he resisted, but then he began

to compromise. He disobediently began to tolerate a more widespread practice of idolatry. This seemingly small step was just the beginning! He should have never compromised what he knew to be right because he eventually became totally involved in idolatrous worship.

Let me put this in today's terms. Let's say you are married but you "innocently" flirt with someone other than your spouse. Then you defend yourself thinking it won't cause any harm. Beware! Once you cross the line of compromise, it gets easier and easier to flirt until it leads you to commit the sin of adultery. What you once thought was innocent is no longer innocent. What you once said you would never do, you've done. The problem? You opened the door to the enemy. You compromised and took a step of disobedience, and before you knew it, you were trapped. That goes for any sin, by the way. Once your resistance is down and you allow compromise to enter your life, you will soon find yourself immersed in sin and serving your flesh rather than God!

In order to avoid the problem of compromise, you must be willing to surrender to Christ. You must let the Lord rule over your every choice. He must be Lord *of* all or He isn't Lord *at* all. He demands complete surrender. You cannot be a Christian that places conditions on the Lord.

It's much like what happened between General Grant and General Lee at the end of the Civil War. Before General Lee would surrender to General Grant, he first told him, "We need our horses and weapons so the men can go home and fend for themselves." Grant's reply was simple, "Unconditional surrender!" Every time Lee tried to ask for other provisions in the terms of surrender, Grant would consistently reply, "Unconditional surrender!" It wasn't until Lee finally agreed to unconditional surrender that Grant then said, "OK, now that you have surrendered unconditionally, let's talk about what you need."

In the same way, the Lord wants unconditional surrender from you! He doesn't want you to give Him all kinds of conditions to your relationship with Him. So many try to bargain with the LORD. That's just not the way it works. He's looking for *unconditional surrender.* Once He sees this, then He supplies all your needs, according to His riches and glory (Philippians 4:19). Is there an area in your life today you're holding back from the Lord, an area that you haven't totally surrendered? It may be some secret or habit or hidden sin. Make the choice to let it go once and for all. In prayer, fully surrender this area of compromise to the Lord and begin experiencing the riches of His glory!

Compromise limits our ability to do what is right.

Have you ever made a decision to compromise because you listened to the voices of others? That is exactly what happened with Pilate, who sent Jesus to the cross. He first heard the "right" voices. His wife spoke to him about a dream she had revealing that Jesus was a righteous man. Next, Pilate's conscience spoke to him saying, "There is no fault in Jesus. He is an innocent man." Then came the voice of compromise—the voice of others. The crowds began to scream, "Crucify Him! Crucify Him!"

Going against what he knew to be true and right, Pilate compromises: "Wanting to satisfy the crowd, Pilate released Barabbas to them. He had Jesus flogged, and handed him over to be crucified" (Mark 15:15, NIV).

Although Jesus was innocent according to Roman law, Pilate caved in to the voices of political pressure. He abandoned what he knew was right. He listened to the angry Jewish leaders and made the decision to go forward with the crucifixion even though his own heart was telling him differently. Compromise always hinders your ability to do what is right.

Consider what voices you are listening to today. Who or what most influences your choices? Are you listening to the opinions of friends, family, or coworkers, or are you listening to God? It's not that you shouldn't listen to others. It's just that you must seek to hear God first. Then you must make the choice to obey Him above all else. I assure you, God will always seek to speak to you. But if you compromise that still, small voice of the Lord, as Pilate did, you cannot possibly do what is right! The evidence of complete compromise may be you saying, as Pilate said, "I wash my hands of this Jesus!"

Laying aside God's clear statements of right and wrong and making decisions based on the preferences or pressures of people will hinder your choice to do what is right, and in the end you will compromise. When times of decision come in your life, purpose in your heart to listen to the Lord's voice above every other voice. Remove yourself from people long enough to hear what the Lord has to say to you. Then do what He tells you to do. Remember, He promises to honor those who do right, not those who make everyone happy.

Compromise can weaken and destroy faith.

Second Corinthians 6:14 (NLT) says, "Don't team up with those who are unbelievers. How can goodness be a partner with wickedness? How can light live with darkness?"

Paul urges believers not to form binding relationships with nonbelievers because this can weaken and destroy our faith. At the very least it will cause us to compromise our Christian commitment, integrity, or standards. To choose to put ourselves in close friendships or partnerships with nonbelievers is spiritually a mismatch. Understand, Paul wants us believers to be active in our witness for Christ to nonbelievers, but we should not partner with them in personal or business relationships because the ultimate consequence could be us compromising our faith.

In my years as a pastor, I can't even begin to count how many people I've counseled who have violated this principle of Scripture. They enter into an unequally yoked relationship fully persuaded that it will somehow work out and that in the end God will be glorified. That's never the case.

If you are a Christian, then you are not to date a nonbeliever in hopes of winning that person to Christ. Worse yet, you are not to marry them. It may start out all fun and loving, but in the final analysis it never works. Trust me, it never works. That's why the Lord set up this standard. He lovingly wants to help you make the very best choices for your life. He wisely instructs you so that you do not have to suffer the miserable consequences of being unequally yoked. The same principle is true for business relationships. You are not to partner with a nonbeliever hoping that your business will thrive. Your standards are different. Your masters are different. In the final analysis, you will either compromise your moral convictions, or there will be a sad and often disastrous split in the relationship. Never forget that Christians do not have the same values as nonbelievers. Therefore, you must avoid choices that cause you to divide your loyalties and weaken your faith.

It is true that you will never spiritually pull someone up to where you are if you are unequally yoked. Instead, you will be pulled down to the other's level. Compromise in any area of your life has serious consequences. It's the first step toward disobedience, and from there, it limits your ability to do what is right and pleasing to the Lord. Ultimately it ends up weakening and destroying your faith. It's not worth it. When you are faced with choices, stop and pray. Read God's Word and ask yourself what it has to say regarding your choice. Seek godly counsel. And above all else, wait on the Lord to show you what to do. Do not take one single step until you know His heart and mind on the matter. Whatever you do, don't ignore what He says! Remember, we are citizens of heaven; therefore, we are to make choices that coincide with the God of heaven.

THE PROBLEM WITH IDOLATRY

Me? A problem with idolatry? Never, you say. Well, allow me then to ask you a few questions: What do you spend most of your time thinking and dreaming about? What do you spend most of your money on? What do you spend most of your time talking about? What drives you? What is your passion? What consumes your thoughts, actions, desires, and heart?

Dr. Martyn Lloyd-Jones once said, "A man's god is that for which he lives, for which he is prepared to give his time, his energy, his money, that which stimulates him and rouses him, excites, and enthuses him."

This statement is a good definition of idolatry. In this day and age, the word *idolatry* often seems to not apply to us because we don't usually see people worshiping animals and other foreign gods in a ritualistic manner, as in biblical times. We tend to think idolatry doesn't relate to us. But it does; it just looks different today. Instead of the worship of idols that took place in biblical times, now people worship money, success, pleasure, career, and even humanity itself! Simply put, idolatry is making the choice to love someone or something more than God and serving that object of love rather than God.

Your answers to the previous questions will be a good indicator as to whether you are completely devoted and committed to God or whether you have a problem with idolatry. Idolatry makes you drift away from the heart of God. When you begin to drift away, you believe that God is no longer sufficient to meet your needs.

This is exactly what happened in the book of Judges. God had continually warned the nation of Israel about worshiping other gods. After generations of drifting and wavering

back and forth, Israel refused to take God's warning to heart.
It was during this time of the children of Israel's idolatry that
they got themselves in dire trouble. So what did they do? As
in the past, they cried out to the Lord for help, but this time
God responded in a very different way. In essence, He said,
"No, I will not help you any longer. Turn now to your gods
for help. You have rejected me and refused to humble yourselves; therefore, I have rejected you this day" (see Judges
10:13-14). It was then the people of Israel realized they could
no longer stand before their enemies without Almighty
God's help. Their idols were absolutely useless! With great
humility, the nation of Israel finally repented of their idolatry.
Then God, because of His great mercy, forgave and delivered
them out of their enemies' hands and back into His graces.

Unfortunately, this is also a real problem today in the
United States. Because of our idolatry, we are no longer able
to stand before our enemies. They mock us openly by removing prayer from our schools; by removing God and His
commandments from government buildings; by forcing us to
remain confined within the walls of our churches and going
no further. We're being defeated as a nation because we have
foolishly turned from God. Our nation that was once her-
alded as "one nation under God" now is more aptly coming
to be known as "one nation under many gods." What a sad
commentary. It is only by God's grace that we are still standing. What can we do? Well, God Himself has told us what to
do in His Word: "If My people who are called by My name

shall humble themselves, and pray and seek My face, and turn from their wicked ways, then I will hear from heaven, and will forgive their sin and heal their land" (2 Chronicles 7:14). But the question remains—will we do what He says?

Satan will often entice believers in subtle ways. Maybe you desire to be accepted, to have a great business, to be married, or to have a child. These things are not wrong. But Satan lures you into believing that you need these things *more* than you need God. And before you know it, you are driven by this need more than you are driven to be close to the Lord.

I remember years ago when I got the urge to buy a soft-top Jeep Wrangler 4x4. I looked and looked until I finally found the one I liked. It was gorgeous! Even the color was what I wanted—gold. There I was, standing and looking at it, justifying all the reasons why I had to have it. I thought to myself, *This is great! I will feel rugged. I will be able to feel the wind blowing through my hair. I will feel young again. I will fulfill a great need inside of my heart.* So, what did I choose to do? I bought it.

Now, nothing against Jeep Wranglers, but for me, this purchase was a joke! Think about it. I stand in the pulpit and teach others that only Jesus can fill the needs in our lives. And there I was, coveting, needing, and longing for a Jeep Wrangler. I really believed for a moment that this vehicle would bring me happiness and contentment. After I bought it, I immediately realized otherwise. As if this were the answer. As if letting the wind blow through my hair was happiness. After all, the reality is that I am bald. I finally reasoned within myself that this vehicle can't make me feel young; I am old. After all, I have a hard time getting in and out of it. To top it all off, I took my wife for a drive, and we went on a ride to the mountains. By the time we got there, both of our necks were sore from all the bouncing caused by the short frame of the jeep. What was I thinking? What had I done? What had I bought? It was then that I named the jeep my "golden calf." Satan had subtly led me to believe a lie, and before I knew it, I had fallen in love with the idea of owning a Jeep Wrangler. Of course, it didn't even come close to satisfying me—idols never do. As soon as I realized my bad choice, I repented and sold the jeep. That was a great day and a valuable lesson in my life. I share this story with you for one reason—so you will realize that anything can become an idol. Idols never satisfy. Nothing can satisfy you except Jesus Christ and Him crucified.

Therefore, you must break the idols in your life. God does not accept competition. Consider this true story. When Mahmud of Ghazni invaded India, his conquering forces entered a celebrated temple to destroy it. Mahmud was entreated by a priest to spare a certain idol, but he refused. Instead, he rained repeated blows upon it. Suddenly the image burst open, and a stream of precious stones cascaded from its hollow interior. In the same way, for each idol you willingly choose to destroy in your life, you will gain more than you lose! Every idol that is demolished brings you new treasures of grace and moves you toward a powerful, more Christlike life.

Over and over in the Old Testament, you will run into what are referred to as the "high places." These were places set aside for idolatry, inappropriate worship, and immoral sexual activities. They were set up at different times throughout the history of both the northern and southern kingdoms of Israel. The kings who built them or chose to allow them to remain never enjoyed total victory and peace in their land. But those kings who chose to demolish these places and tear them down experienced revival throughout their land. What a great motivation for making the choice to once and for all demolish the idols from our own lives. What a great lesson for each of us to learn.

Gideon, a judge in the book of Judges, had to learn this very lesson before God would give him victory in war. The Lord told him to go to his father's house and tear down the family altar, which was for worship to the false god Baal. He was then to replace this idolatrous altar with an altar to Jehovah. Once he was obedient and had done this, God then gave him the victory over his enemies. Similarly for you, true victory only will come when you choose to obey God and remove any idol that stands in the way of your undivided worship to Him.

Now back to my questions at the beginning of this section. Do you have a problem with idolatry? Well, do you value anything more than God? If so, that very thing stands in the way of your relationship with the Lord. God is looking for total consecration. He's a jealous God, and He doesn't want to share the number-one place in your life with anyone or anything else. Idolatry has serious consequences, and it must be dealt with today. If you've allowed something to become a "golden calf," then repent and surrender that thing to the Lord. Remove it if necessary. Now, by faith, choose to put your trust in the true and living God. Give Him back the throne of your heart. By doing this you will experience great victory, and like me, you'll come to realize that only Christ truly satisfies.

THE PROBLEM WITH CARNALITY

What is carnality? Simply put, carnality is a Christian choosing to allow himself to be controlled by his sin nature!

Carnality is a horrible thing, and it's ruining the lives of so many Christians today. It's not an issue of loving the Lord; rather, carnality keeps you away from the goodness, grace, and power that God wants you to have.

Paul aptly describes carnality in Galatians 5:19-21: "Now the works of the flesh [carnality] are evident, which are: adultery, fornication, uncleanness, lewdness, idolatry, sorcery, hatred, contentions, jealousies, outbursts of wrath, selfish ambitions, dissensions, heresies, envy, murders, drunkenness, revelries, and the like; of which I tell you beforehand, just as I also told you in time past, that those who practice such things will not inherit the kingdom of God."

The description of carnality in this passage shows it is fleshly and ugly. If it is not brought under the control of the Holy Spirit, it will literally destroy a person. Unfortunately, carnality is a huge problem within the church today. Many think it is enough to just hear the Word. Not so. We are to be not only hearers but also doers. Each of us must make the choice to allow the Word to enter our heart and then to change us from the inside out.

So what is the solution to carnality? Paul gives the answer to this in the book of Colossians: "If then you were raised with Christ, seek those things which are above, where Christ is, sitting at the right hand of God. Set your mind on things above, not on things on the earth. For you died, and your life is hidden with Christ in God. When Christ who is our life appears, then you also will appear with Him in glory. Therefore put to death your members which are on the earth: fornication, uncleanness, passion, evil desire, and covetousness, which is idolatry. Because of these things the wrath of God is coming upon the sons of disobedience" (Colossians 3:1-6).

Carnality has sobering consequences. If you want victory over it, then you will need to set your mind on Christ. Instead of thinking about what you want or what would feel good to you, think about the Lord and what He asks of you. Make a deliberate choice to keep your thoughts pure, and when they wander, rein them in. When your flesh starts craving things you know are sin, instead of giving in, choose to put to death your flesh. Say no to those sins. Each time you do these things, you feed your spirit. Then it grows stronger, and carnality is purged out of your life.

It's time to consider the consequences of your choices. Compromise. Idolatry. Carnality. These all begin with bad choices. Bad choices lead to bad consequences. No wonder Joshua warned the people: "[Then] he will turn against you and destroy you, even though he has been so good to you" (Joshua 24:20, NLT).

Chapter 9

THE CONFIRMATION

All of us have heard the expression, "Actions speak louder than words." Well, that's what Joshua reminds the people in chapter 24.

> But the people said to Joshua, "No! We will serve the LORD." Then Joshua said, "You are witnesses against yourselves that you have chosen to serve the LORD." "Yes, we are witnesses," they replied. "Now then," said Joshua, "throw away the foreign gods that are among you and yield your hearts to the LORD, the God of Israel." And the people said to Joshua, "We will serve the LORD our God and obey him" (Joshua 24:21-24, NIV).

Simply put, Joshua said to them, "If you are going to make a commitment, then live it! Confirm it by your actions!" The same must be true for you. When you have chosen the Lord, then you must confirm this by your actions. You must prove that you have made a genuine and sincere commitment to the Lord. It's not enough to say that you are a Christian or that you love the Lord; your choices must validate your words. Now, don't get confused. You also can't just run around doing a bunch of good works and because of these declare you are saved. Faith and works go hand in hand. Both are important. Your first choice must be to choose God. From there, the natural outpouring of that choice will be the confirmation of this by your good works.

Choose God

Your life is a sum total of the choices you have made. Whom you choose to serve will impact your life for eternity. Who you are today is because of the choices you made yesterday. Likewise, tomorrow will become the result of today's choices. A successful businessperson and author has said this about choices: "We are free up to the point of choice; then the choice controls the chooser."

The Canadian Northlands experience only two seasons: winter and summer. In the warm weather as the back roads begin to thaw, they become muddy, and vehicles leave deep ruts. Then when winter comes again and the ground freezes hard, these ruts become a part of the traveling challenges. Vehicles entering this undeveloped area during the winter may find a sign posted that reads, "Driver, please choose carefully which rut you drive in because you'll be in it for the next 20 miles."

In my teens and early 20s, my life was in a horrible rut because I had not chosen carefully the path I was taking. Gangs, drugs, violence, and running from the FBI were all bad choices that controlled my daily life and drove me deeper into a mode of destruction. Each awful choice only caused the rut I was in to grow deeper and more impossible to get out of. I stayed in that rut for years until the very grace of God rescued me. By His miraculous deliverance, I was lifted from that rut and put on a whole new highway of life!

One night I'm literally sleeping in the streets and the next I'm sleeping in a Christian home. Through the Lord's hand and His divine deliverance, I ended up in a Christian commune. There in that home, I met a little squirt named Orville. He may have been a man small in stature, but he was mighty in boldness. He faced me head-on and began to give me choices. For the first time in many years, I actually began to make good choices. I handed over my gun, flushed down the toilet what was then $10,000 worth of drugs, and invited Jesus Christ into my life. Once and for all, I chose God. That was my day of decision! From then on I was a new man who was ready to live out a life that confirmed my choice.

That night I made my choice, and suddenly everything clicked. I knew I needed help, and I knew I had exhausted every other option except God. So I chose God. I reached out my hand in desperation, and He just grabbed me and pulled me out of my rut. At the very moment I made the choice to accept Him as my Lord and Savior, He delivered me from drugs, destruction, anger, and a life controlled by my fleshly appetites. I knew I was a new person with a new life ahead of me. With the Lord's strength I formed new habits, and for the first time I had hope. Once a tough and fearless biker, now I chose to sing Christian songs while walking down the street. Looking back I can see that I chose God because He first chose me. Now He is Lord of my life controlling me as He sees fit. It's not that I never make any bad choices, but they are much fewer and farther between these days.

I urge you to choose carefully the path your life takes. Don't make the decision to follow Christ and then try to live on the edge with one foot in Christ's kingdom and one foot in the world. This is a sure recipe for failure. I think you'll better understand this principle through the following illustration.

> The mother of a young boy tucked her son into bed early one night. Afterward, she decided to get some much-needed reading done downstairs by the fireplace. After awhile, she heard a loud thump from the upstairs. Frantically, she ran upstairs, fearing that her little boy had fallen off the bunk bed. When she arrived in the room, to her horror, she did see her son on the wooden floor.

> As she reached down to pick him up, she realized he wasn't crying and wasn't hurt, just a little

shaken up. She comforted him and then tucked him back in bed. The young boy looked at his mom and said, "I guess I stayed too close to the edge of where I got in. This time, I will lay all the way over, next to the wall, and will never lay by the edge of the bed again!"

Perhaps you once chose Christ but you keep falling. Could it be that you've been living too close to the edge of the world? It's never too late to change, but you must make choices that reflect you are all the way into Christ. You can't live on the edge of the world for too long before you fall into sin. The Lord is deserving of your whole-hearted devotion. Stop right now and tell the Lord you want to be devoted completely to Him. Choose God. Ask His Spirit to help you with this choice. When you fail, be quick to repent and make any necessary changes so you will not live life in a dangerous rut. Always be aware that eventually your choices will control you. If you choose to serve the world and other gods, you will eventually reap a life of separation from God and all the consequences for your sinful behaviors. If you choose to serve the Lord, then you will reap eternal life and all the blessings that come from that choice.

Remember that your actions will confirm your choice. If you have truly chosen Christ, then it will be evident that you have a relationship with Him, are walking in harmony with Him, and are serving Him with sincerity! You will find that you are satisfied with Jesus and won't be looking for other things to fill your life. Better yet, the Lord will be satisfied with you. The following poem from an unknown author perfectly illustrates this type of satisfaction:

> I am satisfied with Jesus,
> He has done so much for me,
> He has suffered to redeem me,
> He has died to set me free.
> He is with me in my trials,
> Best of friends of all is He,
> I can always count on Jesus,
> Can He always count on me?
>
> I can hear the voice of Jesus
> Calling out so pleadingly,
> "Go and win the lost and straying."
> Is He satisfied with me?
>
> When my work on earth is ended,
> And I cross the mystic sea,
> Oh, that I could hear Him saying,
> "I am satisfied with thee."
> I am satisfied, I am satisfied,
> I am satisfied with Jesus,
> But the question comes to me,
> As I think of Calvary,
> Is my Master satisfied with me?

I challenge you—it's time to grow. It's time to make choices that reflect you have chosen God. It's time to move closer to the Lord. It's time to be satisfied in Christ alone. Without a doubt, it's time for you to move away from the things that put you on the edge of this world and choose to step wholly into Christ. It's your choice: the floor or a good night's sleep. Which will it be?

HAVING A RELATIONSHIP WITH GOD

Choosing to serve the Lord means having a relationship with God. There are far too many self-professing Christians who say they believe in Christ but have no personal relationship with God. I have met many people who have plenty of head knowledge: They know what the Scriptures say (they can quote them frontward and backward), know the different schools of theology, and even have a good understanding of the Gospel. However, they have no heart knowledge. Simply put, what's in their brain has not reached down into their heart!

When you choose to serve the Lord and commit to Him, you develop a personal relationship with your Maker. All of a sudden, you start to walk in God's footsteps—you look at things through His eyes. In fact, your heart starts to resemble God's heart!

Choosing to have a close, personal relationship with the Lord is vital to serving Him. The more you get to know Him, the more you will fall in love with Him. As you learn to have deep and intimate fellowship with Him, He will become the love of your life, your dearest friend, your Abba Father.

When you have a deep intimacy with the Lord, He takes residence in your heart. You don't treat Him as a guest; rather, you honor Him as the sole owner of your life.

> When Queen Victoria reigned in England, she would occasionally visit some of the humble cottages of her subjects. One time, she entered the home of a widow and enjoyed a brief period of Christian fellowship. A short while later, the poor widow was taunted by her worldly neighbors: "Granny, who's the most honored guest you've ever entertained in your home?" They expected her to say it was Jesus, for despite their constant ridicule of her Christian witness, they recognized her deep spirituality. But to their surprise she answered, "The most honored *guest* I've ever entertained is Her Majesty the Queen." "Did you say the queen? Ah, we caught you this time! How about this Jesus you're always talking about? Isn't He your most honored guest?" Her answer was definite and scriptural: "No, indeed! He's not a guest. He lives here!" Her hecklers were silenced.

Do you have a personal relationship with the Lord, or is He merely a guest that comes and goes as you see fit? The greatest choice you will ever make is to open wide the door of your heart and let Him move in and take over. Once He does that, you will find that you don't have to struggle to make your words and actions line up. Because you have a close and binding relationship with the Lord, you'll naturally want to make choices that please Him. And these choices will confirm your love for Him and help you walk in harmony with Him.

WALKING IN HARMONY WITH GOD

Amos 3:3 says, "Can two walk together, unless they are agreed?"

As a Christian, you must understand that if you are going to walk with God, you must be in harmony with Him! You must walk in step with Him throughout this life by making good and biblical choices. You must be fully persuaded that He is the Lord and you are the servant. He is the Master and you are the slave. He is the Shepherd and you are merely His sheep.

Many Christians are not walking in harmony with God. There is a battle of wills going on. Look at your own life. Are God's way and your own way battling it out? Instead of submitting to God's lordship over your life, are you still demanding your own way? If so, this means you are walking out of step with Him. And believe me, when you are out of sync with God, there will be no harmony inside of you.

And the consequence of this disharmony is nothing but chaos.

First Kings 18:21 says, "How long will you falter between two opinions?"

This should not come as a shock to you, but God's reign in your life is not a democracy! The world has many opinions. It teaches that there are many roads to travel and many ways to get to heaven—*wrong!* Rather, there's only one opinion—God's!

When you are in harmony with God, you are thinking as He does; that is, you are seeking out His will for your life and not your own. Harmony with the Lord means you are choosing to trust Him when things are difficult and not getting impatient when circumstances don't go as you had planned. Walking in harmony with God means you are choosing to live a holy life—agreeing with the Lord regarding the sins in your life and avoiding situations that could cause you to compromise your values.

Living in harmony with God means your words and actions line up! Let me ask you this: When people watch you, when they see the way you behave in public, when they hear your vocabulary while sitting with friends in Starbucks, and when they see how you present yourself—do they see Jesus Christ? Walking in harmony with God means you are choosing to be obedient to His Word! You don't just go through the motions or say you are godly, but your life shows that you really are godly.

The difficult thing in life is being obedient to what you know to be right. The Lord wants harmony with you, and He is telling you to get rid of those things in your life that are sinful and wrong. These things causing disobedience to God (and disharmony) are wiping you out—producing guilt and shame and destroying you emotionally, mentally, physically, and spiritually.

It's time to stop fighting against God. It's time to raise the white flag and surrender. Tell the Lord you are tired of fighting and resisting Him and are ready to choose to walk in harmony with Him today!

SERVING GOD WITH SINCERITY

When you walk in harmony with the Lord, a natural outcome is that you will serve Him in sincerity. This means that your actions will be consistent with your words and you won't be a phony Christian. While reading through this section, I challenge you to examine your heart, your motives, and your actions for serving God. Do a checkup on yourself, like the little boy in this story.

> The pharmacist of the town drugstore overheard a young boy talking on a pay telephone. "Hello, sir, I was calling to see if you needed a lawn boy. Oh, you have one. Well, is he adequate? Oh, he is! Thank you, I was just checking," said the young boy. The pharmacist then said to the boy,

> "Sorry you didn't get the job, son." "Oh, no sir," said the boy. "I've got the job. I was just calling to check up on myself."

If you made a phone call and checked up on yourself, what would those who know you say? Would they say your service is genuine or sincere? Would they say what you do is adequate and fair? The apostle Paul said, "We conducted ourselves in the world in simplicity and godly sincerity" (2 Corinthians 1:12). How are you conducting yourself in the world? God wants you to serve Him with all your heart. He does not want you to serve Him with wrong motives or self-ish ambitions. Rather, He seeks a sincere heart, motivated by love and the desire to be obedient to His Word.

The word *sincere* in the Greek is an interesting word—it means "without wax." In biblical days, when sculptors would make statues out of marble, they would chisel away for years on an image. If there was a flaw or a break, instead of starting over, the sculptor would mix the marble with melted wax and replace the broken piece. No one could tell the difference, but in reality the statue was not molded purely out of marble—it was not *sincere.*

God wants your Christian life to be "without wax." You are not to be living a double standard—serving God when it is convenient but embracing the world at the same time. The Lord wants you to be sincere. He wants you to be the "real deal" and not a fake. He doesn't want you praising the Lord at church and then watching pornography at home. He doesn't want you honoring Him and then constantly gossiping about others. He doesn't want you to dress one way when you come to church and an entirely different way when you're out with your friends. He wants you to be sincere. He wants your lifestyle away from church to be the same as what you present at church. If there's an inconsistency, then you're mixing "wax" into your walk.

Give yourself a checkup. Are you serving God with sincerity, or are there contradictions in your life? Remember, if someone wanted to test the authenticity of a marble statue back then, all they had to do was set it out in the sun. When the temperature rose, the wax would melt and reveal the true condition of the statue.

The same is true for you. What you are made of will be revealed. Through the pressures, heartaches, trials, and suffering of this life, you will be exposed for what you really are. You can fool people for a time but not forever. Eventually the confirmation will come, and you will be known for who you really are. Remember that others are watching your choices and responses to see what you are made of. Be real. Be honest. There's no more powerful testimony than when a Christian man or woman makes the choice to walk in sincerity.

People are looking for some kind of confirmation that you are sincere in your walk. If you're sincere, then others will watch you go through life and faithfully follow the Lord.

They'll see you choose God time after time. They'll see your relationship with Him grow deeper in trust and intimacy. They'll witness harmony between you and the Lord as you accept your circumstances and all He allows to touch your life. Ultimately, they'll desire this kind of sincerity and the freedom that comes from that choice.

Chapter 10

TIME TO MAKE YOUR CHOICE

Life is full of choices. Every day you will be literally bombarded with choices. You will make decisions such as when to get out of bed, what to wear, what to eat, what route to take to work . . . the list just goes on and on. You may look at this partial list and think, *Big deal! What does it matter when I get out of bed or what I wear?* And for most people that kind of reasoning would be absolutely fine. But for the Christian man or woman, the answer is significant.

All of life revolves around *one* choice. When you make the choice to ask Christ into your heart and let Him be Lord over your life, then every subsequent decision, no matter how small or great, will be based on this initial choice.

For example, you have to make a seemingly insignificant choice as to when to get out of bed in the morning. If you're like most people, you set an alarm clock and then proceed to hit the snooze button several times. You eventually peel yourself out from under your covers and head into your day. You get dressed, run out the door, stop by Starbucks or McDonalds, and then most likely get on some freeway that moves at a snail's pace. After several near misses with other drivers and a few cell phone calls, you arrive at work or school barely on time and wearing your breakfast. Your day spins from one thing to the next, and before you know it, you're back on the freeway inching your way home. After weaving in and out of traffic to find the fastest lane and making another dozen or so cell phone calls, you arrive at home just in time to inhale your dinner and get out the door to your next commitment (which you will most likely be late for!).

By now I know you're thinking, *OK, OK, so what's your point?* Remember the choice you had to make as to when you would get out of bed? Well, if you are a Christian, if you love the Lord and want Him to rule over your life, then all of a sudden that choice becomes very significant. Let's say instead of playing tag with the snooze alarm you get up right away. This allows you some extra time to open up your Bible and meet with the Lord. As you read His Word, you find that He begins to prepare you for the day ahead. Now with His Word in you, instead of running all day in the energy of the flesh you can depend on His Spirit to lead you.

From there you'll find that the Lord begins to direct your paths. He gives you words to say (or directs you not to say them), He calms your anxious heart, He protects you, and He gives you strength and confidence. He controls your temper. He gives you victory over temptation, and He literally walks you through your day helping you make good and godly choices. There is nothing—absolutely nothing—He can't do for you! Yet it all begins with your first choice to invite Him into your day by spending some time with Him.

It's time to make your choice: Are you going to serve God or the world?

Joshua said, "[I want you to] fear the Lord" (Joshua 24:14). Joshua made the choice to honor (that is, to fear) God above all else, and his lifestyle reflected that choice. He also wanted others to make this choice because he was certain that it would make all the difference for them. He made his decision to serve God. No matter how much pressure he faced, he stood his ground and declared: "As for me and my house, we will serve the Lord" (Joshua 24:15).

The world we live in today does not fear God. People are not interested in what He thinks of sin. They are not interested in His plans for His people. They are not interested in the life He offers. Instead, people fear what others think of them.

When you fear God, you show reverence to His power and His right to your life. If you possess a healthy fear of God, you will make right choices in your life because you know that separation from God is an eternal condition. As you respect the Lord's ownership over your life—His sovereignty, His grace, and His mercy—you will seek to serve Him with all of your heart and soul.

In this booklet, I have talked about choices. By now you're well aware of the fact that choices do matter. They produce consequences. Good choices equal good consequences. Bad choices lead to difficult and often painful consequences. You cannot just float through life and do what you want with no consideration of the outcome. Today's choices are forming your future. Make no mistake about it—you will reap what you sow.

Joshua challenged the people of Israel to choose whom they would serve. And he further said, "Choose today." Joshua's challenge stands for you today as well. Whom will you serve? If you choose the Lord, then let your life and every choice reflect that decision. I assure you it is the very best choice you will ever make. From the moment I chose Christ, my life has never been the same. Yes, I've had problems and challenges. Yes, I've done things I regret or would do differently today. But through it all Christ has stood with me. He has been that friend who sticks closer than a brother. He has been my guide. He has faithfully led me all the way. Since the day I gave my heart to Him, He has never abandoned me, and I am confident that He will continue to lead me until I am safely home in heaven. Like Fanny Crosby in her hymn, I too declare, "All the way my Savior leads me!" Consider the words to this wonderful hymn:

> All the way my Savior leads me;
> What have I to ask beside?
> Can I doubt His tender mercy,
> Who thru life has been my guide?

Heavenly peace, divinest comfort,
Here by faith with Him to dwell!
For I know whate'er befall me,
Jesus doeth all things well.

All the way my Savior leads me;
Cheers each winding path I tread,
Gives me grace for every trial,
Feeds me with the living bread.

Though my weary steps may falter
And my soul athirst may be,
Gushing from the Rock before me,
Lo! A spring of joy I see.

All the way my Savior leads me;
Oh, the fullness of His love!
Perfect rest to me is promised
In my Father's house above.

When my spirit, clothed immortal,
Wings its flight to realms of day,
This my song through endless ages:
Jesus led me all the way.

You know that the Lord is deserving of your devotion. You have seen that He chooses you, that He delivers you, that He guides you, and that He blesses you! Furthermore, there are choices, consequences (compromise, idolatry, and carnality, which all hinder your commitment to God), and confirmations to be made.

Today is your day of decision. It's time to make your choice. You can't stay neutral; that's impossible. He wants you to choose Him. He wants to lead your life every step along the way. My prayer is that if you don't know Jesus as your Lord and Savior, you will make the choice to invite Him into your heart and life today. It's so simple. You're just a prayer away.

Perhaps you once made a commitment to Jesus yet you've made a series of bad choices that have left you far away from the Lord and walking out of harmony with Him. You know that your life is not sincere. Jesus knows this too. My prayer for you is that you will make the choice to return to your first love. I assure you that Jesus is waiting to embrace you the moment you turn back to Him. He'll not only cleanse and forgive you, but He'll also strengthen you to once again walk hand in hand with Him.

If you're a Christian and you love the Lord today, may He continue to strengthen you by His Holy Spirit to make good and godly choices. Stand strong and continue to fight the good fight of faith. Don't listen to the lies of the enemy, and don't let anyone move you to take even the smallest step in the direction of compromise.

Choose Christ. Choose life. There's no other way to be happy. My heartfelt cry is that each one of you will one day be able to look back over your life and joyfully declare with me, "Jesus led me all the way!"

Will you pray with me right now?

> Dear Jesus, I invite You to be the Lord of my life. I choose You! Remove compromise from my life. Help me begin every day by meeting with You, through Your Word. Let my lifestyle reflect my commitment to You.
>
> I pray that I will honor and fear You reverently and that You will keep me from sin. *Deliver* me from evil. *Guide* all my steps and *bless* me through Your grace and mercy, as I cling tightly to Your promises.
>
> Thank You for choosing me!
>
> In Jesus' Name, Amen.

MATERIALS AVAILABLE BY STEVE MAYS

A HEARTBEAT FROM HELL
The Steve Mays' Story

At one point in life, Steve Mays was desperate, hopeless, and sleeping in the gutters; he was living with a group of guys twice his age, who were involved in motorcycle gangs. A 38-caliber bullet had penetrated his left leg. The FBI had a warrant out for his arrest regarding a recent shooting. Then one day something happened; it was as if Steve was a new man. His whole life changed.

How can God love a desolate man full of anger and wrath? How can God take an addict and make him an obedient God-fearing pastor? How can God use us to His fullest if we are weak or disabled?

―――――

We encourage you to visit Calvary Chapel South Bay's website at www.ccsouthbay.org if you want to order additional copies of *Choices* or Steve Mays' testimony, *Heartbeat from Hell*. If you wish to receive additional information and audio messages by Steve Mays (video/audiotape, CD packages, and Bible studies), these are also available online or you may contact us by calling 310-352-3333 or by writing to:

Calvary Chapel South Bay
19300 S. Vermont Avenue
Gardena, CA 90248